Things That Go!

HOW TO MAKE TOY BOATS, CARS, and PLANES

Written by Judith Conaway

Illustrated by Renzo Barto

Troll Associates

Library of Congress Cataloging in Publication Data

Conaway, Judith (date)
· Things that go!

   Summary: Provides directions for making seventeen
toy boats, cars, and planes, including such special
vehicles as a milk-carton ferryboat and a toothpaste-box
airplane.
   1. Toy making—Juvenile literature.   2. Vehicles—
Models—Juvenile literature.   [1. Toy making.
2. Vehicles—Models.   3. Handicraft]   I. Barto, Renzo,
ill.   II. Title.
TT174.5.V43C66   1987   745.592   86-7130
ISBN 0-8167-0838-X (lib. bdg.)
ISBN 0-8167-0839-8 (pbk.)

10   9   8   7   6   5   4   3   2   1

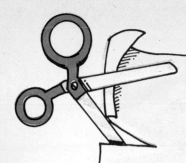

CONTENTS

TINY RACING CAR

Here's what you need:

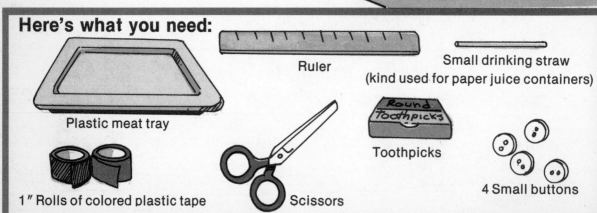

Ruler

Small drinking straw
(kind used for paper juice containers)

Plastic meat tray

Round
Toothpicks

Toothpicks

4 Small buttons

1″ Rolls of colored plastic tape   Scissors

Here's what you do:

1 Cut out a 3-½ " × 1-¼ " rectangle from a clean plastic tray. Trim off two corners at the dotted lines.

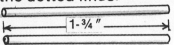

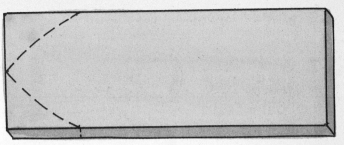

2 Cut a small drinking straw into two pieces, each 1-¾ " long. Tape each length of straw to the plastic, as shown.

3 Insert a round toothpick through each straw. Place a button on the ends of each toothpick. To hold each button on, wrap a small strip of tape around the tips of each toothpick.

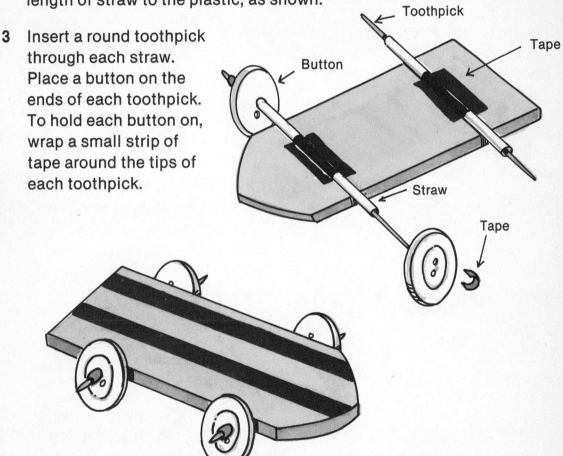

4 Turn the racer over. Use colored plastic tape to add some racing stripes to your car. You can make your racer go with just a push of your finger. The button wheels actually turn. Make a few racers and have a race!

JET-PROPELLED RACING CAR

After you have made the racing car on page 4, add this idea. Watch your racer really go! You will need a small balloon, a piece of poster board, and some tape.

1 Cut a rectangle of this size out of poster board.

2 Cut an X, as shown. Fold up the poster board along the dotted line. Then place a small piece of tape over the top of the cut.

3 Slip the open end of the balloon through the slit.

4 Add two strips of colored tape across the poster board, and tape it to the body of the racer.

5 Blow up the balloon. Then hold the air in the balloon by pinching it closed with your fingers. Place the racer on a flat surface and release the balloon. Watch the racer zoom!

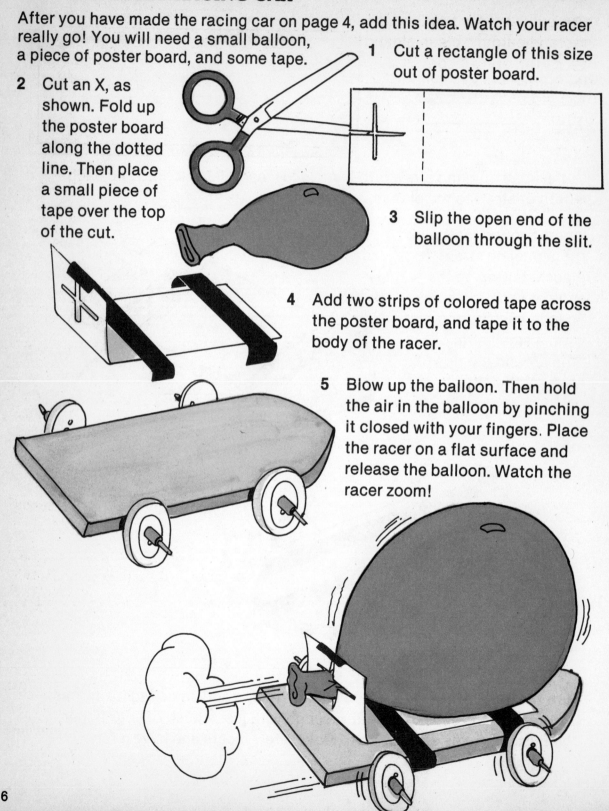

PLASTIC SAILBOAT

With the same materials used to make the car on page 4, plus some heavy paper, a pushpin, and nail polish, you can make a sailboat!

1 Cut out a piece of plastic of this size and shape. Make a small hole where shown.

3/8"

2 For the mast, cut a small straw so it is 2-½" long. Insert a pushpin through the straw, as shown.

3 Carefully insert a toothpick through both holes. Center the toothpick.

4 Cut out this sail shape from a sturdy piece of paper. Make three holes where shown.

5 To assemble the boat, slip the top of the mast into the top hole of the sail. Carefully slip each end of the toothpick into the other two holes. Insert the bottom of the mast into the boat. Put a drop of nail polish into the hole to hold the mast in place.

6 Float your boat in a pan of water or in a sink. Point a straw at the sail and blow through it.

KOOKY CAR

Here's what you need:

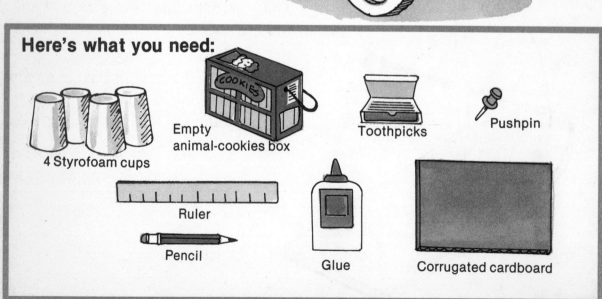

4 Styrofoam cups

Empty animal-cookies box

Toothpicks

Pushpin

Ruler

Pencil

Glue

Corrugated cardboard

Here's what you do:

1 Remove the string handle from the box. Cut away part of the flap and the two sides, as shown.

2 Cut a strip of cardboard small enough to cover the bottom of the box. (Be sure to cut against the ridges.) Put the cardboard in the box.

3 Use a pushpin to make four holes in the box, two on each side, as shown. Each hole should be about ¾″ from the bottom and the sides of the box.

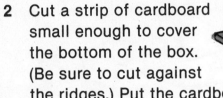

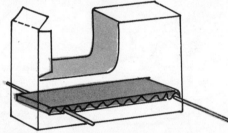

4 Insert a toothpick into each hole and through the ridges of the cardboard within the box.

5 Fold and glue the box flap and tabs A and C. Fold tab B up to form the windshield.

6 Cut off the bottoms of four styrofoam cups to make the wheels.

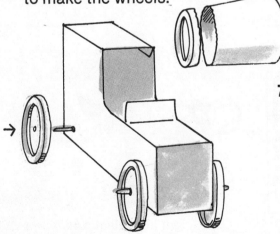

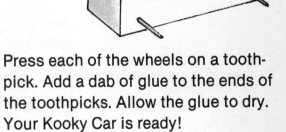

7 Press each of the wheels on a toothpick. Add a dab of glue to the ends of the toothpicks. Allow the glue to dry. Your Kooky Car is ready!

9

MILK-CARTON FERRYBOAT

Here's what you need:

Empty matchbox
(kitchen-match size)

Markers

Empty quart-size milk carton

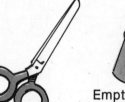

Scissors

Empty container
from roll of film

Spigot from plastic container

Here's what you do:

1 Rinse and dry the empty milk carton. Cut out a ferryboat shape, as shown.

2 Cut the matchbox to fit on top of the ferryboat. Draw windows and doors on it. Cut a small round hole on top, and insert the plastic spigot in it. Glue the matchbox to the top of the boat.

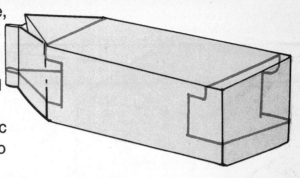

3 Glue the empty film container to the boat, as shown. It forms the smokestack.

4 Use markers to add details, such as portholes and trim.

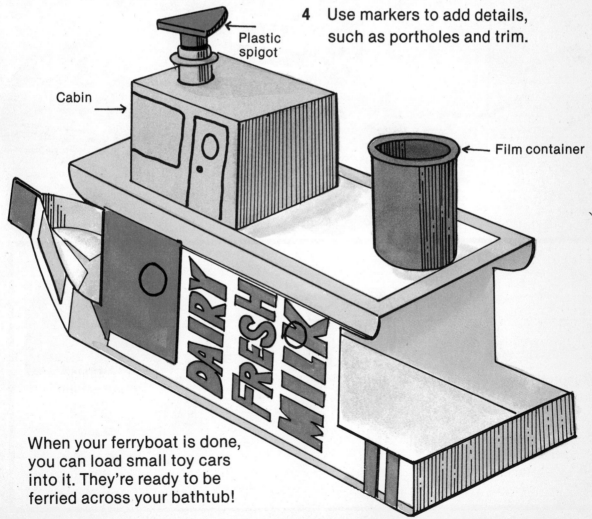

Plastic spigot

Cabin

Film container

When your ferryboat is done, you can load small toy cars into it. They're ready to be ferried across your bathtub!

OATMEAL-BOX TANK TRUCK

Here's what you need:

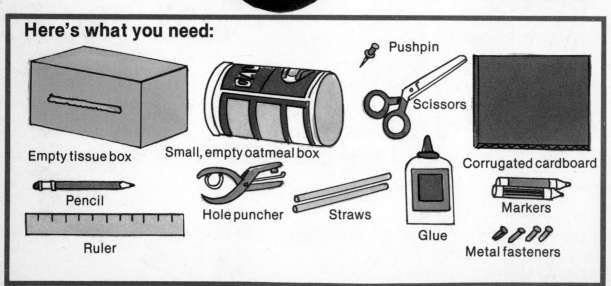

Empty tissue box

Small, empty oatmeal box

Pushpin

Scissors

Corrugated cardboard

Pencil

Hole puncher

Straws

Glue

Markers

Ruler

Metal fasteners

Here's what you do to make the cab and body:

1 Cut the tissue box along the red lines, as shown. (*Note:* The distance from A to B should be the same as from C to D.)

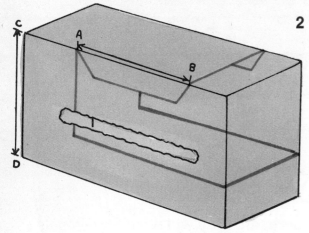

2 Fold along the dotted line to form the front of the truck. Glue the tabs closed.

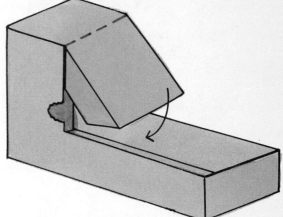

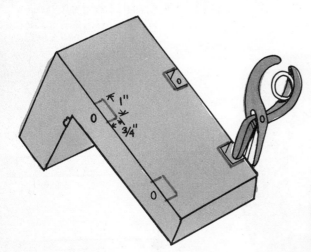

3 Turn the tissue box over, and mark the bottom of the box, as shown. Carefully cut along the red lines and fold the tabs up, inside the truck. With a hole puncher, make a hole through both layers of each tab.

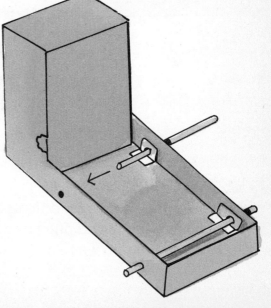

4 Insert a straw into each set of holes to make the axles.

(Turn the page for more directions.)

Here's what you do to make the wheels:

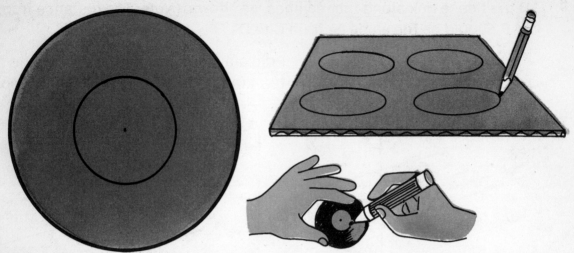

1 Copy the wheel pattern onto a piece of cardboard. You will need four wheels. Cut out each circle.

2 Make a hole in the center of each wheel, by first making a small hole with a pushpin. Then carefully put the pointed end of a pencil into the hole. Gently push the pencil through to enlarge the hole so that a straw will fit snugly into it.

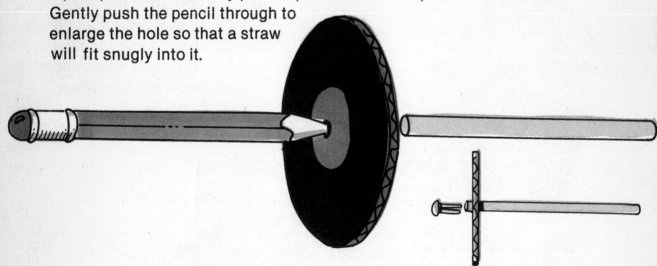

3 To attach the tires, push one onto each end of the straws. Open a small metal fastener slightly and push into the opening of each straw. Do the same for the rest of the wheels. The fasteners will keep the tires from falling off.

To finish the truck:

1 Apply glue to both ends of the oatmeal box. Place the oatmeal box in the tissue box, as shown. Let the glue dry completely.

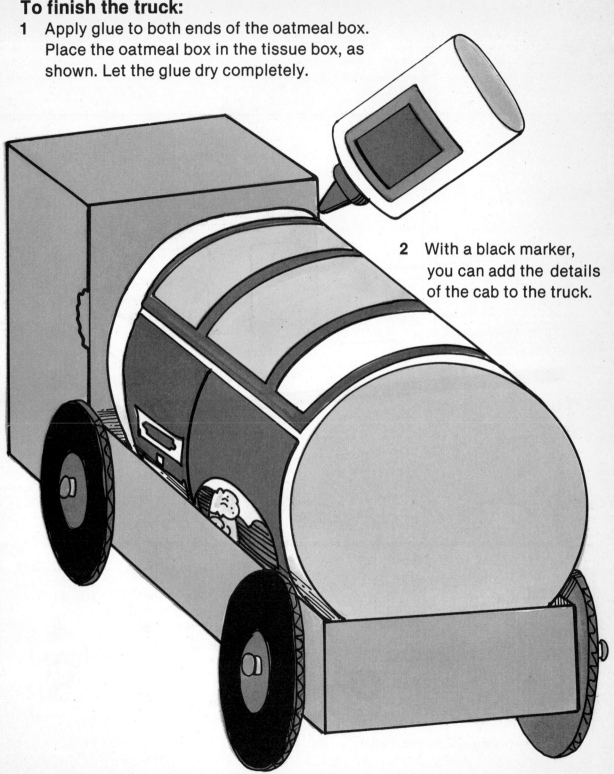

2 With a black marker, you can add the details of the cab to the truck.

STYROFOAM TUGBOAT

Here's what you need:

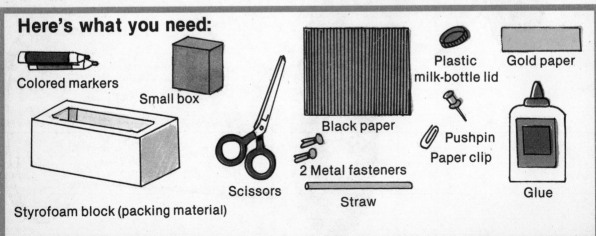

Colored markers

Small box

Black paper

Plastic milk-bottle lid

Gold paper

Scissors

2 Metal fasteners

Straw

Pushpin

Paper clip

Glue

Styrofoam block (packing material)

Here's what you do:

1 Use a styrofoam packing block for the hull. Add a small box for the cabin. The box should fit snugly in the hull.

2 For the smokestack, roll a piece of black paper into a tube. Glue it closed. Cut a circle out of the top of the cabin. Put the smokestack into the hole. Wrap a band of gold or yellow paper around the smoke-stack, and glue in place.

3 Push two metal fasteners into the front of the cabin, as shown.

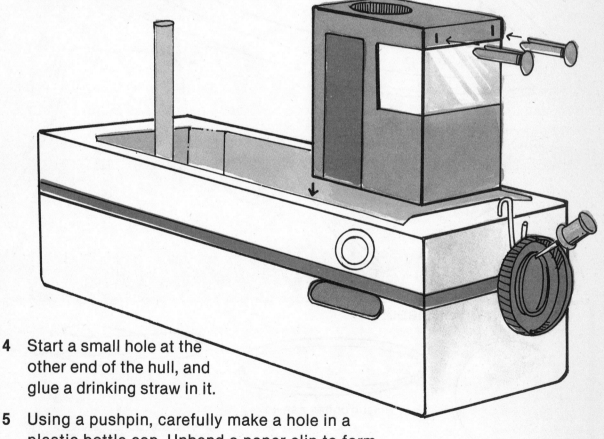

4 Start a small hole at the other end of the hull, and glue a drinking straw in it.

5 Using a pushpin, carefully make a hole in a plastic bottle cap. Unbend a paper clip to form a hook. Place one end of the paper clip into the cap and hook the other end to the styrofoam, as shown.

6 Use markers to add the details of the tugboat.

FLYING SAUCER

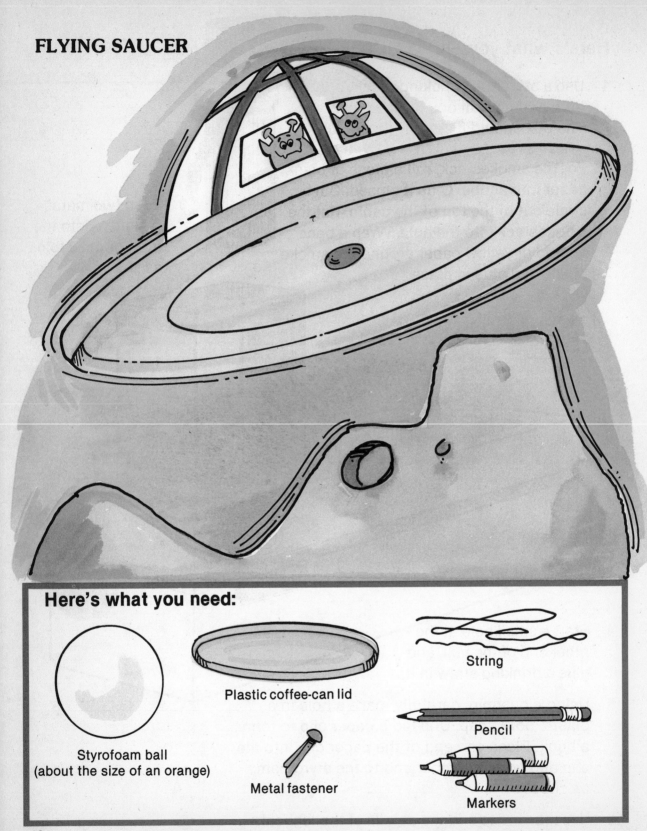

Here's what you need:

Styrofoam ball
(about the size of an orange)

Plastic coffee-can lid

Metal fastener

String

Pencil

Markers

Here's what you do:

1 To cut the styrofoam in half, tie a string around the center of the ball. Slip a pencil between the string and ball. Turn the pencil around and around. As you turn, the string will tighten and cut the ball in half.

2 Use the tip of a metal fastener to carefully punch a hole in the plastic lid. Poke the fastener through the hole.

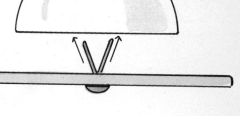

3 Open the fastener so that the points are spread about ¼" apart. Press one half of the styrofoam ball down onto the fastener.

4 Decorate your flying saucer with markers. Follow this design or create one of your own.

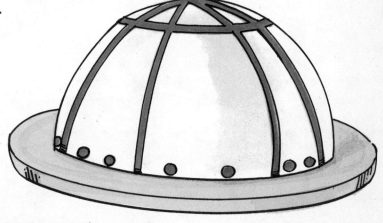

5 Now go outside and give your flying saucer a backhand toss. Watch it whirl through space.

WEATHER WHIRLYBIRD

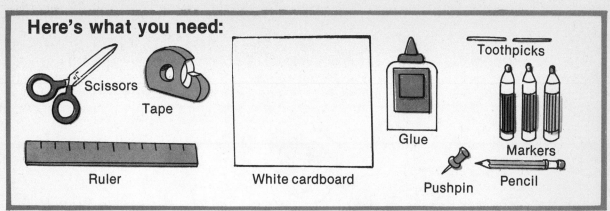

Here's what you need:

Scissors
Tape
Ruler
White cardboard
Glue
Pushpin
Pencil
Toothpicks
Markers

Here's what you do:

1. Copy this pattern for the helicopter blades onto cardboard. Carefully make a small hole in the center with a pushpin.

2. Cut out the blades. Use markers to color the blades. (Remember to color both sides.)

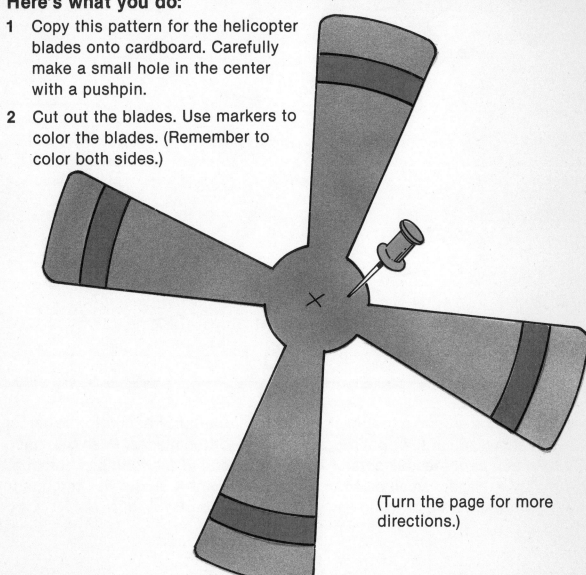

(Turn the page for more directions.)

3 Copy the helicopter pattern shown here onto cardboard. Carefully cut it out. Fold along all dotted lines. Glue all tabs in place. Allow glue to dry.

4 Using a pushpin, make four small holes at points A, B, C, and D.

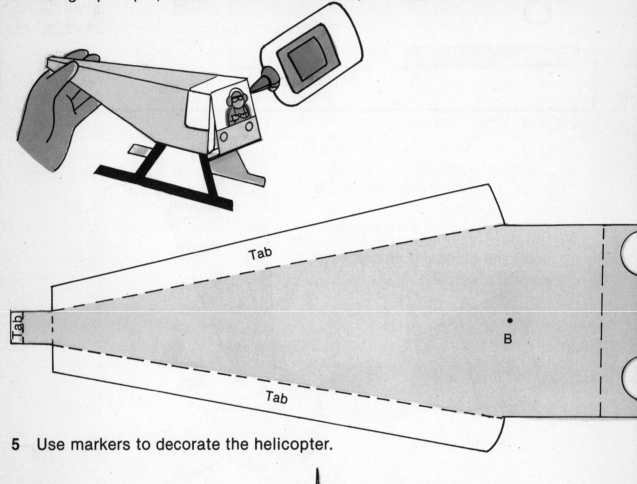

5 Use markers to decorate the helicopter.

6 Wrap tape around a toothpick, as shown. Push the tip through the center of the helicopter blades. Place a small piece of tape over the tip of the toothpick and onto the center of the blades. Push the other end of the toothpick through point A all the way through to point B.

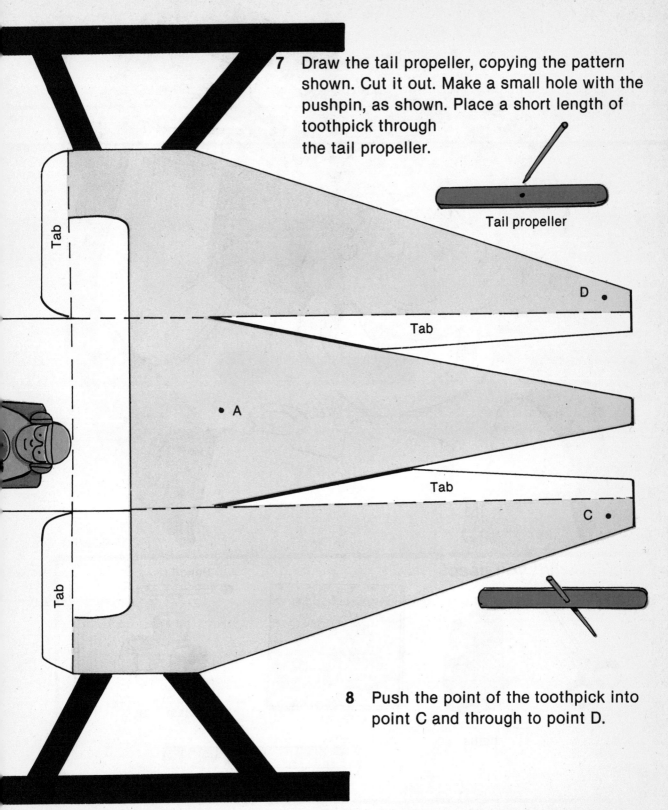

7 Draw the tail propeller, copying the pattern shown. Cut it out. Make a small hole with the pushpin, as shown. Place a short length of toothpick through the tail propeller.

Tail propeller

Tab

Tab

D

Tab

A

Tab

C

8 Push the point of the toothpick into point C and through to point D.

SPACE SHIP

Here's what you need:

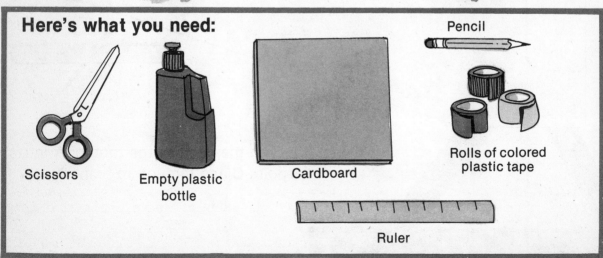

Scissors

Empty plastic bottle

Cardboard

Pencil

Rolls of colored plastic tape

Ruler

Here's what you do:

1 Copy the pattern for the wings onto cardboard. Cut the wings out.

2 Using scissors, carefully make a slit on each side of the empty plastic bottle. Slip the wings into the slits.

Use white tape for cockpit.

Add stripes on sides.

3 Cut out strips and pieces of colored plastic tape and put them on the bottle and wings. You can use the design shown here—or you can make up one of your own.

Add stripes and an insignia on wings.

Your space ship is now ready for outer-space travel!

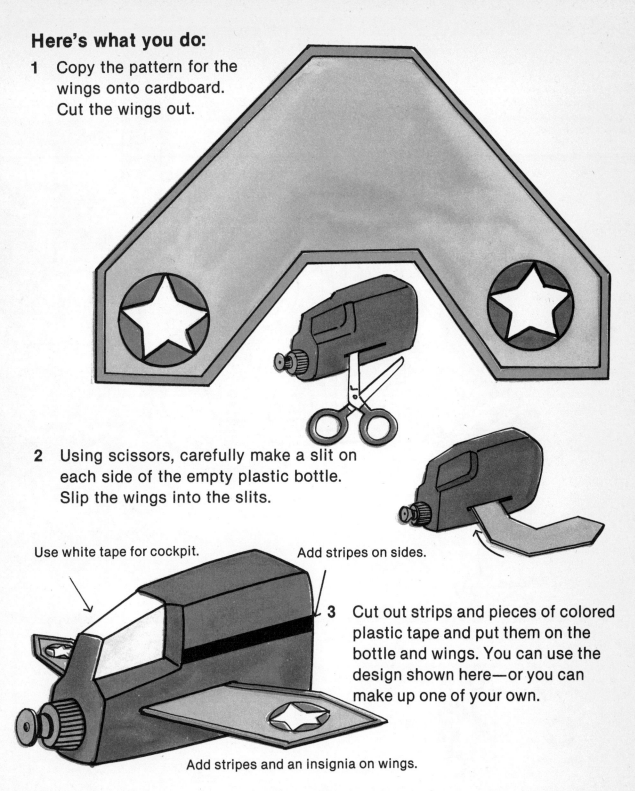

FIRE ENGINE

Here's what you need:

Scissors

Markers

Pushpin

Metal fastener

Toothpick

White cardboard

Corrugated cardboard

Pencil

Ruler

Glue

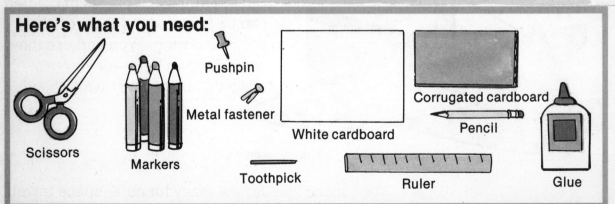

Here's what you do:

1 Copy the ladder pattern onto white cardboard.
Cut out the shape carefully.

2 Color the ladder with a black marker. Fold
down the tabs. Make two small holes with
a pushpin, where shown.

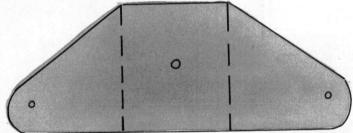

3 Copy this shape on a piece of corrugated cardboard, and cut it out.
Make two small holes and one larger center hole with the pushpin.
Fold along the dotted lines.

4 To assemble the ladder and swivel,
place a toothpick through one
folded tab of the ladder. Then push
the toothpick through both tabs of
the swivel, and finally through the
other tab of the ladder.

Note: The metal fastener shown here will go
through the center hole of the swivel onto the
body of the truck.

5 Copy the truck shape on a sheet of white cardboard. Carefully cut out the truck. Fold all tabs and fold along all dotted lines. Color the truck with markers.

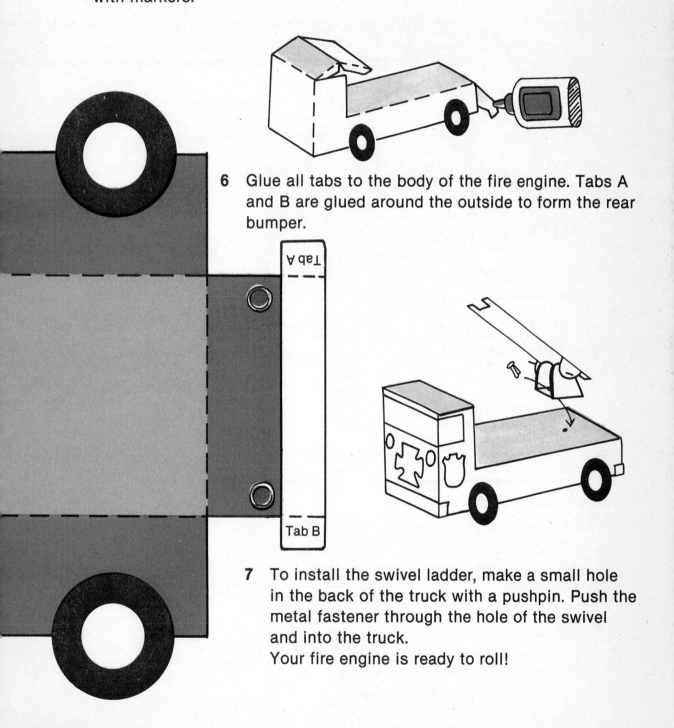

6 Glue all tabs to the body of the fire engine. Tabs A and B are glued around the outside to form the rear bumper.

Tab A

Tab B

7 To install the swivel ladder, make a small hole in the back of the truck with a pushpin. Push the metal fastener through the hole of the swivel and into the truck.
Your fire engine is ready to roll!

SEDAN

Here's what you need:

Poster board Scissors Glue Pencil Markers Ruler

Here's what you do:

1 Carefully copy the car pattern shown on the next page onto a sheet of poster board. Cut out the car, including the tabs. Use markers to color your sedan. Outline all parts in black.

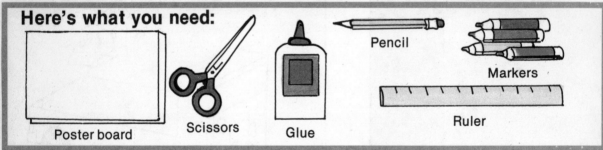

2 Fold along all dotted lines. Apply glue to the tabs, refold the car, and let the glue dry completely. *Note:* The bumpers and windshield are glued around the outside of the car.

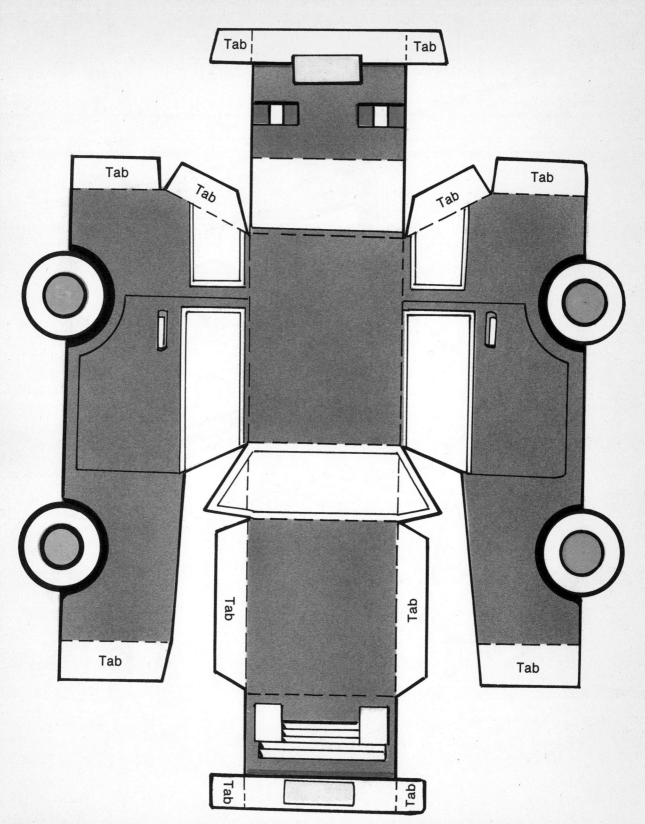

CABLE CAR

You can make your own overhead cable car. Turn the page to find out how!

Here's what you need:

Poster board

Scissors

Pencil

Cord

Glue

Hole puncher

Crayons

Ruler

Here's what you do:

1 Copy this pattern onto poster board. Cut it out. Fold along all dotted lines. You can cut out the windows or draw them in, using crayons.

OVERHEAD CABLE CAR

Tab

Tab

2 Add details, and color the cable car.

3 Use a hole puncher to make two holes, where shown.

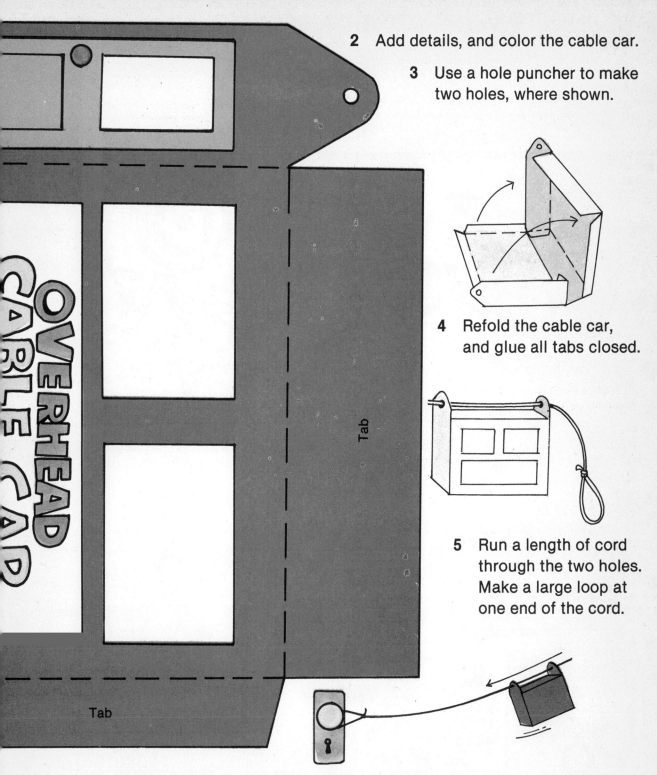

4 Refold the cable car, and glue all tabs closed.

5 Run a length of cord through the two holes. Make a large loop at one end of the cord.

6 Hook the loop over the doorknob. Raise the other end of the cord, while holding the cable car. Release the car and see it speed down the cable!

TOOTHPASTE-BOX AIRPLANE

Here's what you need:

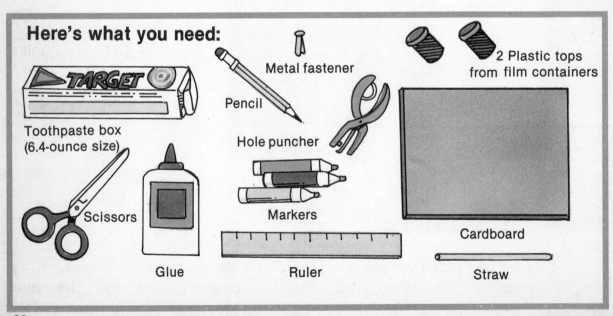

Toothpaste box
(6.4-ounce size)

Scissors

Glue

Pencil

Hole puncher

Markers

Ruler

Metal fastener

2 Plastic tops
from film containers

Cardboard

Straw

Here's what you do:

1 Make a ½" long slit at one end of the box.

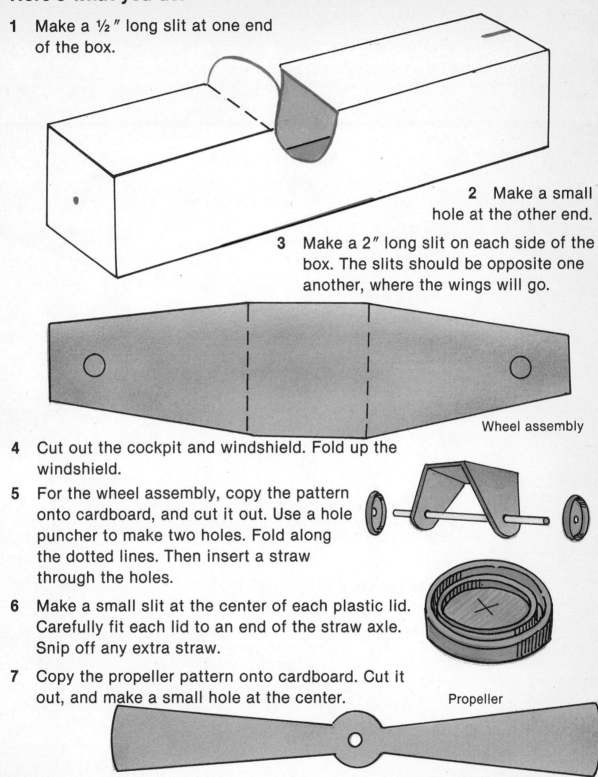

2 Make a small hole at the other end.

3 Make a 2" long slit on each side of the box. The slits should be opposite one another, where the wings will go.

Wheel assembly

4 Cut out the cockpit and windshield. Fold up the windshield.

5 For the wheel assembly, copy the pattern onto cardboard, and cut it out. Use a hole puncher to make two holes. Fold along the dotted lines. Then insert a straw through the holes.

6 Make a small slit at the center of each plastic lid. Carefully fit each lid to an end of the straw axle. Snip off any extra straw.

7 Copy the propeller pattern onto cardboard. Cut it out, and make a small hole at the center.

Propeller

8 Copy the wings, tail, and stabilizer onto cardboard. Cut out each piece. Decorate the sections with markers, adding stripes, stars, or anything you like.

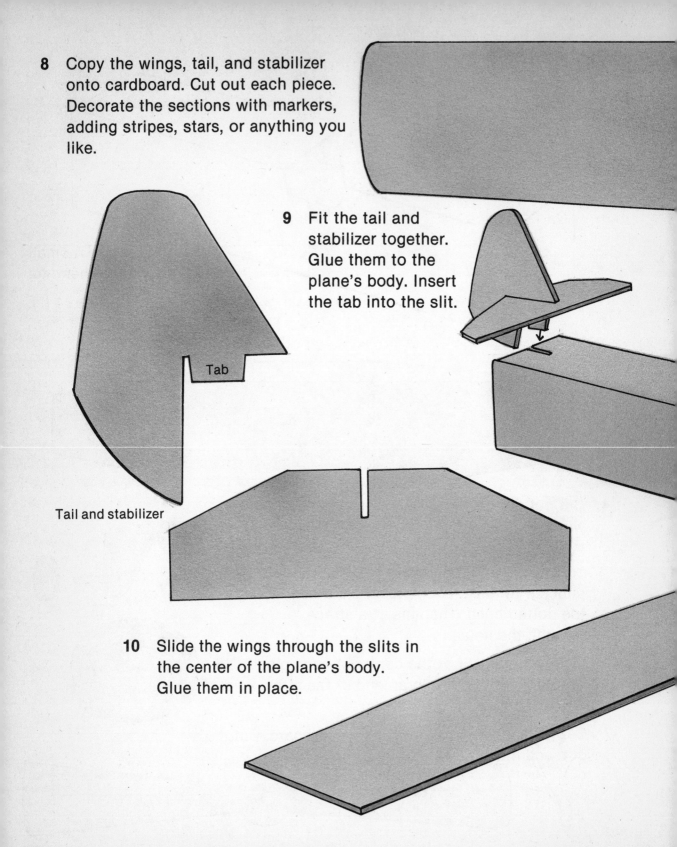

9 Fit the tail and stabilizer together. Glue them to the plane's body. Insert the tab into the slit.

Tab

Tail and stabilizer

10 Slide the wings through the slits in the center of the plane's body. Glue them in place.

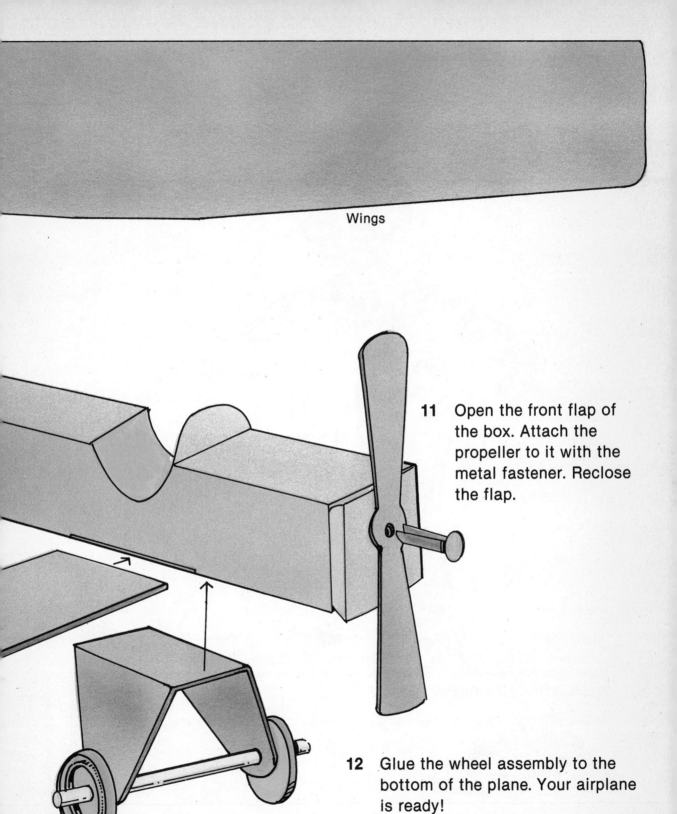

Wings

11 Open the front flap of the box. Attach the propeller to it with the metal fastener. Reclose the flap.

12 Glue the wheel assembly to the bottom of the plane. Your airplane is ready!

OLD-FASHIONED PAPER PLANE

Here's what you need:

Crayons

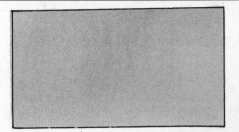

Paper clip

Paper

Here's what you do:

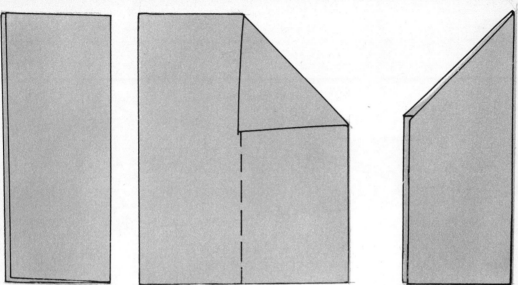

1   Fold a sheet of paper in half. Open it out flat. Fold a corner down, so it touches the center line. Fold the other corner the same way. Fold the paper in half again. This is the nose of the plane.

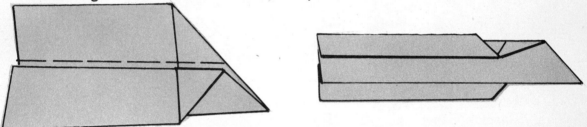

2   To make the wings, fold down each side more than halfway. Then fold each wing back up to the center fold, as shown.

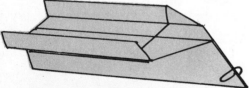

3   Open the last two folds you made so that the wings stand up. Place a paper clip at the nose of the plane. It will help the plane to balance.

4   If you like, decorate your plane with crayons.

5   To fly the plane, hold it as shown. Then toss the plane with a smooth overhand motion. Watch it fly and loop about!

SUPER-GLIDER PAPER PLANE

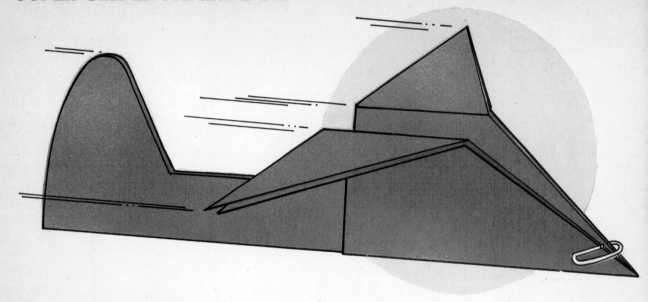

Here's what you need:

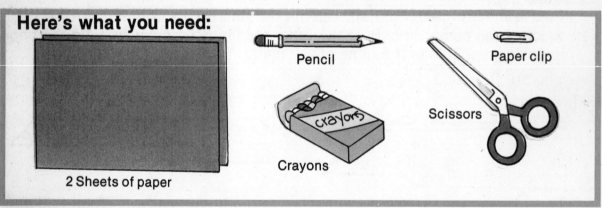

2 Sheets of paper

Pencil

Crayons

Scissors

Paper clip

Here's what you do:

1 Fold a square sheet of paper in half, diagonally. Then fold it in half again, diagonally.

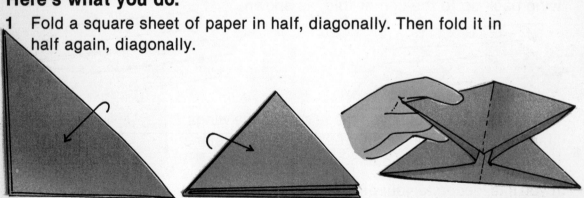

2 Open the sheet, and refold it as shown.

3 To make the body of the glider, fold the other sheet of paper in half, lengthwise. Copy this pattern onto it. Cut out the shape, cutting through both layers.

4 Use crayons to decorate your glider.

5 Place the body shape into the lower fold of the wing shape. Then fold up the wings and body shape.

Fold line ⟶

6 Fold the tips of the wings down, on both sides. Add a paper clip to the nose of the glider, and you're ready to soar!

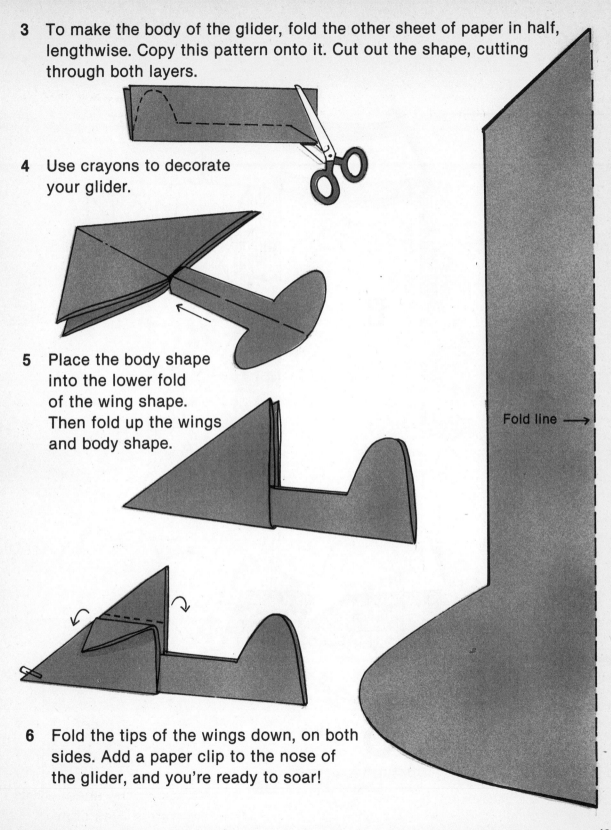

ROCKET

Here's what you do:

1 To make the nose cone, copy this half circle onto a piece of stiff paper. Cut it out, and roll it into a cone shape. Glue together the areas that overlap.

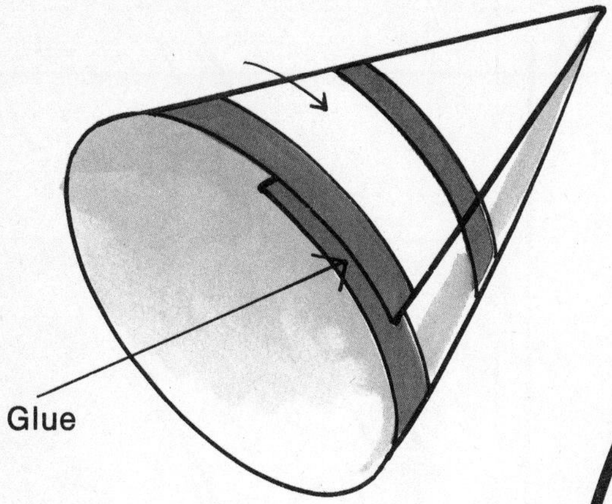

Glue

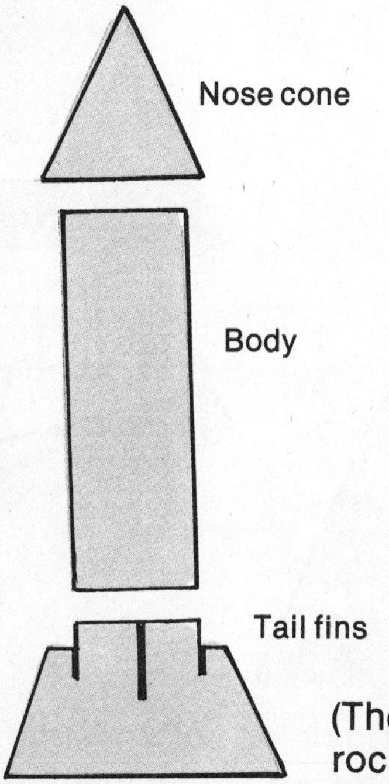

Nose cone

Body

Tail fins

(The patterns for the rocket's body and tail fins are on the following pages.)

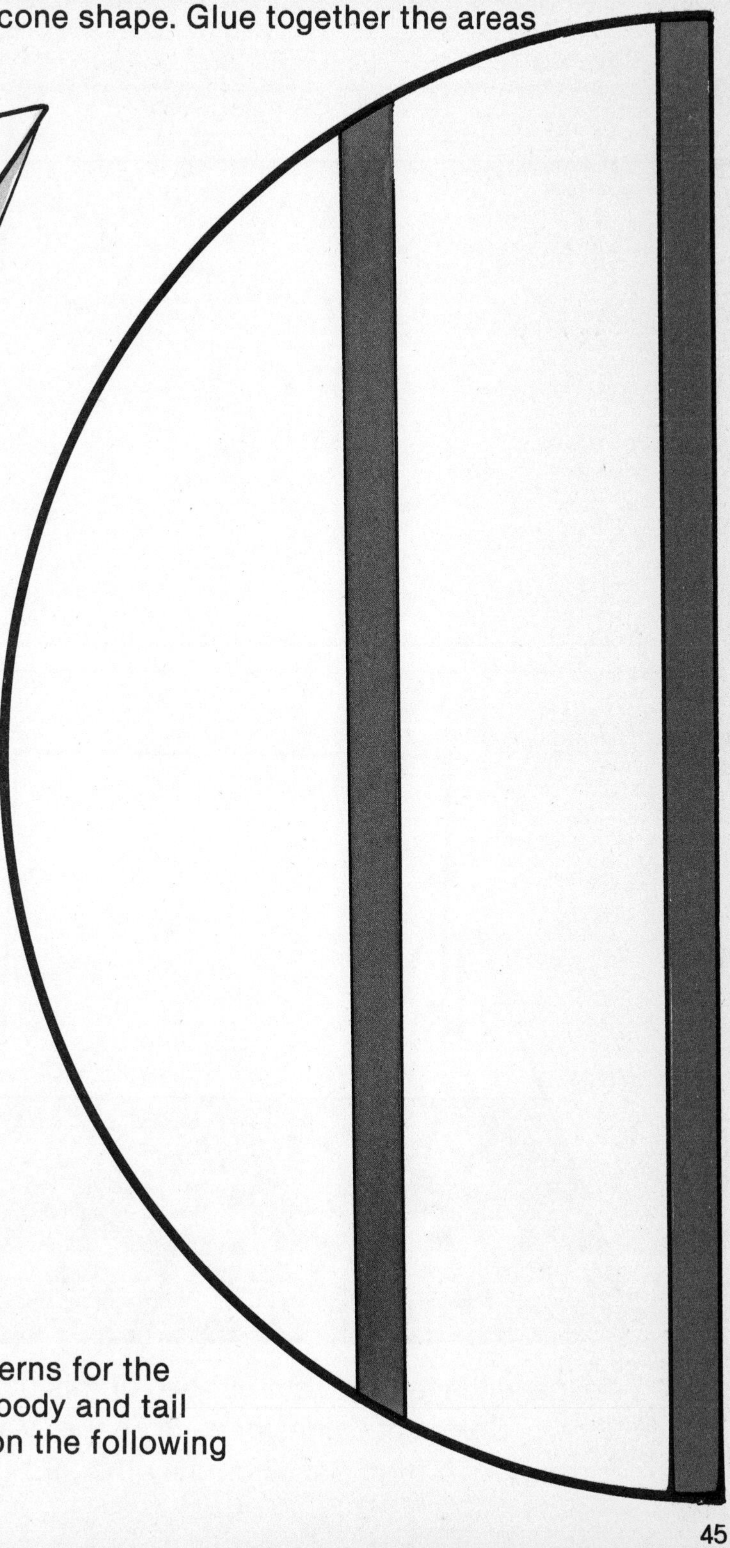

2 To make the rocket's body, use a sheet of stiff paper (about 7-½″ × 9″). Apply glue along one end, as shown. Roll the paper into a tube, so its diameter is 2-⅜″.

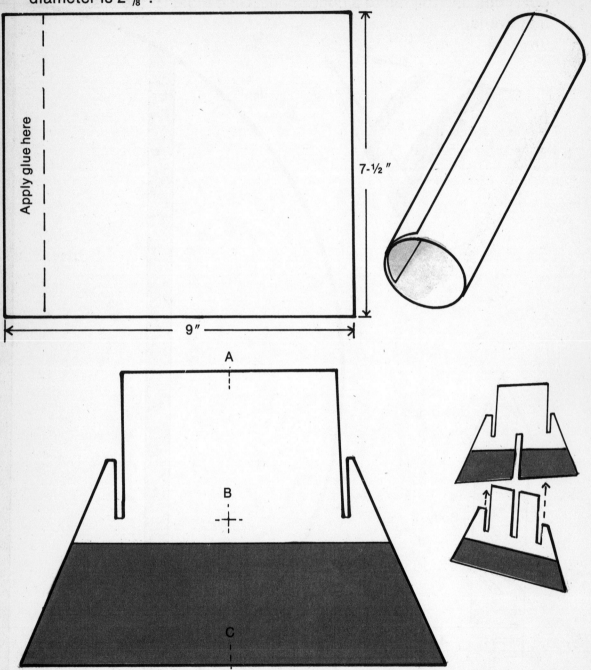

3 To make the tail fins, cut out two of this pattern. Color the bottom strip, as shown. Color both sides of each shape. Make a slit from points A to B on one fin, and a slit from B to C on the other. Fit the two pieces together.

4 To assemble the rocket, cut a series of slits around one end of the tube, and fold down the tabs. Apply glue to the tabs, and glue the cone to the tabs.

5 Use crayons to decorate the body and nose cone.

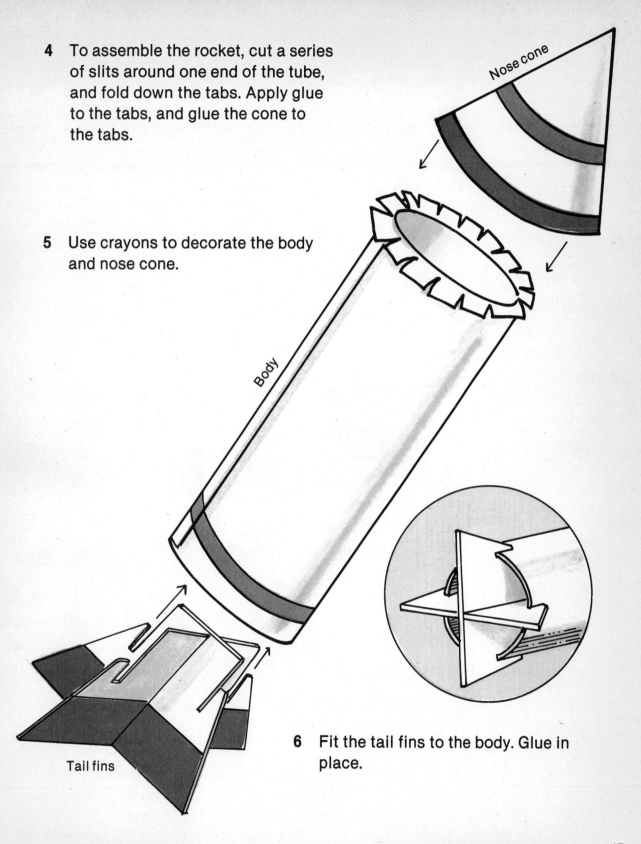

Nose cone

Body

Tail fins

6 Fit the tail fins to the body. Glue in place.